Nehru Bal Pustakalaya

ISON's Journey

Idris Siddiqui

Illustrations
Arup Gupta

nbt.india
एकः सूते सकलम्
NATIONAL BOOK TRUST, INDIA

High up in the sky, there were silver-dust clouds spread all across. From among these clouds, ISON came out. He was seen moving very fast. Looking at his speed, it wasn't difficult to say that he was going on a long journey.

“Where is this ISON going at such a great speed?” Pollux asked his friend Castor, who was at a distance. Pollux was shining the brightest.

“On a long journey, perhaps,” said Castor looking at the fast-moving ISON. Like Pollux, Castor was also so bright that it almost appeared blue in white light. Residing in the sky, Pollux and Castor were neighbours.

"ISON can do anything!" said Pollux laughingly.

"Of course," Castor replied, "He is a bit crazy."

By that time, ISON had moved far away from there. He was not worried about what Pollux was saying.

"ISON isn't grown enough to travel long distances."

"Ah, poor ISON!" added Castor, sadly. "He is just six kilometers long. Don't know what will happen to him?

"But ISON has a lot of courage," Pollux said praising the far-moving ISON.

ISON was only thinking about becoming immortal in the skies and on Earth. His journey was so long that it would take him millions of years and even for that, he had to travel at a great

speed. Otherwise, his life would be over but not the journey. This was how far he had to go.

"There is a lot of load on my back. Carrying all this means I can't move speedily," ISON thought to himself and he wasn't wrong in thinking so. He was weighed down by heavy boulders of soot and ice that he carried on his back.

"I must get rid of some of the weight to gain speed," decided ISON. Every minute, he shed five thousand kilos of dust and sixty-five kilos of water. ISON threw dust and ice from the boulders loaded over his back.

"How to melt and shed the ice?" ISON was thinking of a way to get rid of the ice boulders. They also weighed a lot. Otherwise, he would not be able to reach his maximum possible speed.

Suddenly, he smiled as a thought ran through his mind.

"I will have to get to the Sun's boundary. There the Sun's heat would be effective," this thought encouraged ISON. The boundary began at a distance of 2.5 to 3 million miles from the Sun.

"There my problem would be solved," ISON spoke to himself on the long journey. He was alone after all.

That is what happened. ISON's idea turned out to be successful. "It's good that the boundary falls on my way. Otherwise, I would have had to travel extra," ISON was pleased to think about this.

The things on his back heated up as soon as ISON entered the Sun's boundary. The region where there were boulders of dust and ice started boiling. It was good that they turned into small particles and flew away. The ice heated up and the water particles formed a thin sheet and covered him. Now he had a covering of vapours all around him.

ISON immediately took a decision, “To enhance my speed, I will have to get rid of gas and dust,” he sighed in relief as he left them both behind. The gas and the dust looked like a tail behind him. The solar wind blew both tails back. ISON was surprised to see that the thinning tails turned out to be one hundred eighty-six thousand miles long!

After getting rid of a lot of weight, ISON, high up in the sky, was able to attain great speed. From a distance, ISON looked green because of his tails. He was convinced that he would certainly complete his journey.

He was not worried about what would happen. ISON was crazy indeed!

As ISON got closer to the sun, his speed increased. Earlier he was behind the Sun. But that day, he was not just facing the Sun, he was very close to it. The fearless ISON was now actually quite near the Sun.

There, the extreme heat gave him a very hard time, even though he was still 1.2 million kilometers away from the Sun's core. That much heat is enough to melt iron. But ISON kept going. So much so that he got burnt by the Sun's flames. However, that also didn't stop him and he reached the Sun. That is where ISON met his end.

The comet ISON died but went on to live forever.

*ISON reached the Sun on 28 November 2013 and met his end there.